RENT TO RENT

MULTI LET CASHFLOW, PASSIVE INCOME SYSTEM USING AIRBNB, BOOKING OR LONG TERM RENTALS

LARRY HARWOOD

stanfordpub.com

FOREWORD

It has been suggested that a "rent-to-rent" arrangement is a quick and simple route to huge passive income for property investors. You sign a contract, you accept a payment upfront, and your tenant takes responsibility for the property.

Sounds fantastic! With such an apparently easy method of making profit with minimal hassle and effort, it is no wonder that the practice of rent-to-rent is becoming popular in the ever-changing business of property investment.

While there is undoubtedly an appeal to opening your property to a rent-to-rent tenancy, such agreements have suffered a sprinkling of bad press. Claims of unethical practice and properties being left in a poor state have appeared online and in newspapers, leaving many property owners hesitant to even contemplate a rent-to-rent arrangement.

Rent to rent is a topic that has been broached and referenced on Facebook Community numerous times, which has revealed that there are no doubt misconceptions as well as hurdles to consider before committing. Let's discuss the draws and the drawbacks, the pros and the cons, with the aim of helping you decide whether the quick and easy appeal of rent-to-rent might be for you.

What is rent-to-rent?

Rent-to-rent is when you rent out a property to a tenant on a single let basis. This tenant will rarely live at the property, and will be free to sub-let its rooms as they see fit. Depending on the type of property and the agreements made, sometimes the arrangement involves a small amount of refurb work, converting offices/lounges etc into extra bedrooms. Some rent-to-rent sub-letters will ask for financial help from the property owner in order to make these adjustments.

The sub-letter will then rent out the property to (usually 4+) separate tenants while paying the property's single let rent and bills, while pocketing the difference.

Why would you agree?

The shrewd property investors among you might ask, "Why would I work hard to purchase my properties, build up a great portfolio, and then allow other entrepreneurs to dive in and make more than me?"

It's certainly a valid question, but we are very keen on the idea of passive income. Being a landlord can also be a stressful role, meaning that when presented with such an opportunity, plenty of people leap at the opportunity for several years' guaranteed rent all at once. In a rent-to-rent scenario, property owners are guaranteed a specific start date, with no empty periods for however long the agreement lasts, plus no missed or late payments due to them being paid in lump sums.

Many of the time-consuming aspects of renting out a property are taken care of by the sub-letter, meaning that you, as the property owner, do not have to handle tenant queries or day-to-day management responsibilities and can rely on the sub-letter to deal with the smaller maintenance issues.

Essentially, you are receiving the asking price of your rent AND scraping a whole pile of hassle off your plate.

Misconceptions about rent-to-rent

• Rent-to-rent is not an assured shorthold tenancy

Because the tenant is not going to be living in the property, it cannot be considered an assured shorthold tenancy, and should not be treated as such. Such agreements will be commercial or business tenancies.

• Tenants cannot be evicted without a court order

Just because the property is being sub-let, a tenant still has their right to remain at the property, and they cannot be removed without the presence of a court order. Evicting a tenant without a court order is a criminal offence, and landlords/sub-letters who try it risk being taken to court for damages.

• A rent-to-rent agreement is not a licence, and neither are those of the live-in tenants

The sub-letting tenant will have a contract with you for their part in the renting and upkeep of the property, and the tenants living there are likely to have assured shorthold tenancies, even though they are sub-letting through a 3rd party. This means that all rights that generally go along with renting a property are likely to be in place, despite the primary arrangement being between owner and sub-letter.

So, could rent-to-rent be for you?

As with any change in your property investing strategy, the most important thing to bear in mind is putting in your due diligence. While no one would deny the attraction of what appears to be 100% passive income, there have been criticisms and questions raised that you will want to carefully consider beforehand.

If you are curious about rent-to-rent there are many resources online that you can research from, which will include both the positives and the negatives of the practice, both of which you should pay careful attention to. Ask yourself, will you be content knowing that while you are making money from your portfolio, someone else may be profiting from your hard work? Do you want more or less control over your tenants' living environments, bearing in mind that comfortable tenants are more likely to be good tenants? Are you certain about the legal implications of rent-to-rent, and are you confident in the legitimacy of the sub-letter?

I am excited to share with you my success plan that led me from having no property experience and being stuck in a corporate job to freedom with over £100,000 profit from Rent to Rent properties in only 12 months.

The key topics we are going to cover are as follows:

1. Understand Your Goals & Create a Business Plan
2. Setup Your Business (Legalities)
3. Research Your Goldmine Area
4. Turning on Your Marketing Machine
5. Setting Up Your Systems
6. Finding Your Power Team
7. Taking ACTION!

I'd love to understand why you are interested in Rent to Rent. So if you have a second please respond to this email and let me know what has drawn you to Rent to Rent. For me it was because I wanted to generate cash flow quickly so that I could leave my corporate job as soon as possible and be able to do whatever I wanted - whenever I wanted to do it. I'm still working towards complete freedom but I'm definitely living a dream life! What about you? Let me know why you are doing Rent to Rent!

CHAPTER 1

Are you ready to get started?! I'm super excited you are joining us and I hope you are ready for Step 1 of the Rent to Rent Success Plan. So grab a cuppa and your notepaper and get ready to supercharge your Rent to Rent Business.

Step 1: Understand Your Goals & Create a Business Plan

This is the step that many people leave out when they get started. They are in such a rush to find a property that they don't think they need to have a plan or set goals. But how do you know where you are going unless you have a plan. Like using a sat nav when you drive. If you don't put in a destination the sat nav can't calculate a route. This is the same in your life and your rent to rent business. You need to know where you want to be and what your personal plan is in order to start executing it.

So I suggest you break this step down into a few smaller steps:

1. Understand your reason why. What is your purpose in starting a rent to rent business. And this isn't just to make money. What is the purpose of that money? Is it to spend more time with your family? To have extra holidays? To be able to quit your job? Why are you doing this? And make sure it's powerful as you are going to need to come back to this when times get tough - and they will! Because although Rent to Rent is simple when using the 7 steps, it isn't easy and there will be times when you will want to quit. But if you have a strong vision of what your future will be then you will be able to keep focus and keep going!

2. Understand your financials. Where are you at currently. What is your personal cash flow like right now? Are you earning more than you spend each month? Or are you spending more than you earn? What are you spending your money on? This can be a really eye opening exercise if you have never done it before. And you don't need to go into a lot of detail - just a few lines on what is going into

and out of your bank account each month and how much is left over.

3. Then building on your personal cash flow, you need to understand what you want it to be. Most people skip this step as well and just pick a number out of thin air and say - I want £5,000 a month or I want £10,000 a month. And these are great numbers and definitely achievable...but do you really want them? What will you spend that money on? So take some time in this step to imagine your dream life. Imagine if you had everything you wanted. The beach house and the London flat, Your country home and 1st class flights for all of your holidays. Don't forget the Bentley and Porchse for the driveway? How much for your children's education? Now look at all of those things and make them into monthly figures. How much will you need to pay monthly to lease or buy those cars? What about leasing or paying the mortgages on those dream homes. Remember you don't need to buy them upfront and they are often a lot less than you think they are. So get on Rightmove and car financing websites, check out the cost of universities to see what the real cost is and how much you really need per month to live the life of your dreams. It's even cheaper if you want that life to be someone exotic like Bali, or Thailand as the cost of living is so much lower. Can you imagine

spending every day at the beach with your own personal bartender to make your favorite concoction? It's all possible - so just spend the time to see how much it really is to make that happen.

4. Now using what you've done above, put that into an overall business plan. Again, this doesn't have to be long or detailed, but just an overview of what you want to do and where you want to go. Our business plan started off as a basic 2 phase plan. Year 1 - Rent to Rent in Oxford. Target Income of £100k per annum. Year 2 - Purchase properties with JV partners. Target 4 properties per year with a minimum ROI of 20%. There were a few more details than that, but not much.

Once you've got your goals and business plan sorted out - you should have a clearer idea of the What and the Why. In the next chapters we will get into the details a bit more with Step 2: Setup Your Business (Legalities). The next lesson is all about contracts, insurance, redress schemes to make sure you do it properly!

CHAPTER 2

Setup Your Business (Legalities)

Like I mention before - Rent to Rent is a property business. You don't own the properties you are simply managing them, for an excellent profit. This is a business and you need to treat it as such. Therefore you need to set it up legally!

I don't have time to go into all the details of limited company vs. sole trader and you don't need to get into that much detail at this point. You can run your Rent to Rent business either way and there are pros and cons of each. Talk to an accountant if you want more information.

But I suggest you just pick one and get started. If you've never managed a business or a limited company before, it's probably easiest to start as a sole trader as there is a lot less paperwork. You can always transfer over to a limited company later. If you do have experience with a limited company or maybe you already have a limited company that you work through, great - then consider using that one and just get started! Don't make it any more complicated than that in the beginning as you can always change it later. Just pick one and get started.

What else do you need to do? Well, no matter what business structure you choose there are some more key steps.

1. Public Liability Insurance. Now that you are running a business, whether a limited company or sole trader, you need insurance public liability insurance at a minimum. There are different levels and different types of cover so a good insurance broker will be able to help.

2. Register with a Redress Scheme. As of October 2014 it became mandatory for anyone managing properties in the UK, that they don't own to register with a Redress Scheme. There are currently 3 options:

    a. The Property Redress Scheme (https://www.theprs.co.uk/)

    b. The Property Ombudsman (https://www.tpos.co.uk/)

    c. The Ombudsman - Property Services (http://www.ombudsman-services.org/property.html)

Again - don't spend a lot of time here. They are all very similar. Some have different insurance and setup requirements. And there are slightly different cost structures. I recommend you have a look at each of their websites and then just pick one and go for it. If you don't like it, you can always change next year.

3. Register with the Information Commisioners Office under the Data Protection Act . The Data Protection Act of 1998 requires everyone who processes personal information to register with the ICO. For instance, you process personal data if you handle anyone's phone number (think landlords and tenants). That means we will all qualify as part of a Rent to Rent business because you will need to contact and track both landlords and tenants. It's only £35 per year and a legal requirement so get on it (https://ico.org.uk/)

4. Get a Business Bank Account. Again - even if you are running your business as a sole trader you should have a separate bank account that your Rent to Rent monies will be going through. This should be completely separate from your personal bank account. You will want to be able to track your Rent to

Rent business separately so that you know if it is profitable and so that you can easily identify all your costs and incomings. If you have a limited company you are required to have a business bank account not just a separate personal account. Personally, I think this is just to increase the profits of the banks as they all charge extra for business banking.

Those are the basic steps for business setup. There are of course other things to consider and everyone's personal circumstances are different. For instance there may be other insurance requirements for your business or other accounting or tax implications depending on your personal circumstances. Ensure you speak with the proper professionals in these areas and we will cover a bit more about them in Chapter 6.

CHAPTER 3

Now we that we've put the foundation in place with Chapter 1 & 2 (make sure you read them and action them if you haven't already) we can start actually looking at properties type stuff! I am sure this is what most of you were waiting for. But I hope you didn't just skip the first 2 chapters as they are super important. Don't worry, I'll wait here while you go back and finish them if you haven't already!

....................waiting.....................

Great, now you are ready to move on :)

So let's jump into finding your Goldmine Area!

Research Your Goldmine Area

I believe that it is always best to focus on one area to start with. You can always expand later but for now try to pick one centre of operations. For my business - I looked around the closest cities to where I live (Oxford, Swindon, Reading, Gloucester) and ended up choosing Oxford based on my area research.

Here are a few things you should be looking for:

Tenant Demand - Are there enough tenants looking for HMO type accommodation to keep your rooms filled? This is the most important step as if you don't have tenants you won't have income. You can have all the properties in town but without tenant demand you are doomed. So put some test adverts up on Spareroom, Gumtree, newspapers or wherever else local tenants look for housing and see what they are looking for and how many of them are looking!
I love using Spareroom for testing tenant demand. They have a great feature that allows you to see how many rooms are

available in an area vs. how many tenants are looking for rooms. To see how many rooms are available simply do a search as a tenant would. On the home page in the search bar put in your city or post code and select "Rooms for Rent" and press the Search Now button and note down the number of results. Then to see how many tenants are looking for a room go back to the search box on the home page and enter your city or postcode again and this time search for "Rooms Wanted" and note down those results. Ideally, the Rooms Wanted will be higher than the Rooms Available. If not, you may need to dig deeper and really understand if this is a good area as there may not be enough rental demand.

This is a rough, high level test. There are a lot of other factors at play here but it's a good, quick indicator if you should spend more time researching an area or not.

Competition - While you are putting up your test adverts, check out other landlord's adverts. What kinds of rooms are they advertising? Check out the pictures to see the standard of the accommodation. Understand their prices and the location of the other HMOs in the area. What services and utilities are they including in the rent and what other benefits are they offering? The more you understand about your competition the more laser focused you can be on making sure your houses are just a little bit better than theirs so that you attract the best tenants.

Public Transport - Many people living in HMOs won't have cars. So they will need to travel via public transport. It's important to understand what is available in your area. Are there buses, trains, underground stations? Even look at bicycle paths. Make sure your tenants will be able to get to and from work and to the shops easily and safely.

Local Amenities - Where are the local shops? How far away are they? Where are the local employers? What about gyms? Think about it from your preferred tenants point of view. What would they want to live near? Young professionals like restaurants and bars, students want to live close to the university. Make sure the required amenities are nearby.

Tenant type - Another key thing to think about is what type of tenant do you want? Are you looking to have students? Professionals? DSS / housing benefit? Maybe you want to focus on hospital workers. Generally it's best to pick one type of tenant for each house as mixing tenant types can cause more personality conflicts and more house upset. And unhappy tenants make running a profitable Rent to Rent business difficult. Also - if you want to house students, make sure you are in a student area. Same with hospital employees - make sure there is a hospital nearby :)

CHAPTER 4
Marketing

This is a must have activity and focus point for any business and especially for your Rent to Rent business. If you don't have your marketing machine running you won't be getting any properties. This doesn't have to mean you are doing super expensive ads and leafletting campaigns, marketing can be as simple as you getting out and speaking to agents. So it can be super simple, but a lot of people fail to do it - I know you won't be one of them!

In this lesson I'm going to give you a load of different options that you can apply in your Rent to Rent business. You don't have to do all of them but mix and match and test them out to see what works the best for your and your business (and your budget).

Turning on Your Marketing Machine

So now that you know your area from Chapter 3 you are ready to start marketing. So Chapter 4 is to get your marketing machine turned on. There are many different options for marketing, so I'll run through a few of them. You can choose to do all of them or just pick and mix. Find what works best in your area.

I categorize marketing into 2 main areas. Direct to Landlord and Indirect. Let's cover indirect first as it's the quickest to get up and running, but often takes a little longer to get results.

Indirect Marketing

Indirect means going through letting agents and you generally aren't speaking directly to the landlord. This method can get you out and looking at houses a lot more quickly than direct marketing so I highly recommend it (it can take a while to setup newspaper ads and start mailing letters). Using this method means you will have to focus heavily on building relationships.

So this option is quite simple. Get on RightMove

or get out to the high street and start talking to agents. Start checking out the properties that are available and talking to the agents about what you are looking for. You'll want to build up rapport and slowly explain to them what you are doing. There may be a lot of objections at this stage, especially when you first start out. But the more agents you speak to and the more often you speak to them the more confident you will become. Don't worry about them saying No. A No doesn't mean No forever. It just means they don't understand how you can work together and it means that you haven't built up enough rapport with them yet. So get out and look at as many properties as you can with agents as you won't ever get any Rent to Rent's if you don't look at properties! And make sure you take the time to understand the agent, their business and how they work so that you can show them how you can help them to reach their goals and help their clients (ie. the property owners) to meet their goals so that everyone has a win-win situation.

Direct Marketing

The other method of marketing is direct to landlord. This can take a bit longer to setup so is good to get started right away and then speak to agents (like we just discussed above) while you are waiting for the landlords to start calling. Normally you need 5 to 7 points of contact with a landlord (according to different marketing companies) before the landlord will reach out. Sometimes it's more and sometimes it's less. So that's why it's good to employ a combination of the following methods. And it's also good to do each one more than once or keep them running for a minimum of 6 months before switching or giving up. In fact, never give up, make an educated and business focused decision that the method isn't working for you.

- Newspaper Ads - we've had great success with our newspaper ad. A simple ad drawing the attention of the landlord saying something like: Attention Landlords - We can rent your house for 3-5 years. Guaranteed Rents is perfect!
- Flyers / Postcards in shop windows. You'd be surprised how many people read all those flyers and advertisements in shop windows. So walk through your target area and pop into the local

shops and ask them if you can advertise there. Most of them are around £1 per week. Again - keep it simple like in the newspaper ad and use bright colours that will stand out.

- Direct to Landlord letters. This is a more advanced method so we won't go into all the details, but all you need to do is contact your local council for their list of licensed HMOs and their owners. Then you can mail them directly asking if they would be interested in long-term guaranteed rents.

Those are the top forms of marketing that I recommend and have used myself. Keep calm and pick one or two to focus on. And also make sure you don't switch and change too often. Marketing can take some time to build momentum and is all about building trust with your potential clients. I recommend you get a direct marketing method up and running and while that is in the background gaining momentum - get out there are build relationships with agents!

In the next Chapter we are going to be focusing on my other favorite topic: Setting Up Your Systems. I'll give you some great tips on a few key metrics you should be tracking and easy ways to track them!

Marketing

This is a must have activity and focus point for any business and especially for your Rent to Rent business. If you don't have your marketing machine running you won't be getting any properties. This doesn't have to mean you are doing super expensive ads and leafletting campaigns, marketing can be as simple as you getting out and speaking to agents. So it can be super simple, but a lot of people fail to do it - I know you won't be one of them!

In this lesson I'm going to give you a load of different options that you can apply in your Rent to Rent business. You don't have to do all of them but mix and match and test them out to see what works the best for your and your business (and your budget).

Turning on Your Marketing Machine

So now that you know your area from Step 3 you are ready to start marketing. So step 4 is to get your marketing machine turned on. There are many different options for marketing, so I'll run through a few of them. You can choose to do all of them or just pick and mix. Find what works best in your area.

I categorize marketing into 2 main areas. Direct to Landlord and Indirect. Let's cover indirect first as it's the quickest to get up and running, but often takes a little longer to get results.

Indirect Marketing

Indirect means going through letting agents and you generally aren't speaking directly to the landlord. This method can get you out and looking at houses a lot more quickly than direct marketing so I highly recommend it (it can take a while to setup newspaper ads and start mailing letters). Using this method means you will have to focus heavily on building relationships.

So this option is quite simple. Get on RightMove or get out to the high street and start talking to agents. Start checking out the properties that are available and talking to the agents about what you are looking for. You'll want to build up rapport and slowly explain to them what you are doing. There may be a lot of objections at this stage, especially when you first start out. But the more agents you speak to and the more often you speak to them the more confident you will become. Don't worry about them saying No. A No doesn't mean No forever. It just means they don't understand how you can work together and it means that you haven't built up enough rapport with them yet. So get out and look at as many properties as you can with agents as you won't ever get any Rent to Rent's if you don't look at properties! And make sure you take the time to understand the agent, their business and how they work so that you can show them how you can help them to reach their goals and help their clients (ie. the property owners) to meet their goals so that everyone has a win-win situation.

Direct Marketing

The other method of marketing is direct to landlord. This can take a bit longer to setup so is good to get started right away and then speak to agents (like we just discussed above) while you are waiting for the landlords to start calling. Normally you need 5 to 7 points of contact with a landlord (according to different marketing companies) before the landlord will reach out. Sometimes it's more and sometimes it's less. So that's why it's good to employ a combination of the following methods. And it's also good to do each one more than once or keep them running for a minimum of 6 months before switching or giving up. In fact, never give up, make an educated and business focused decision that the method isn't working for you.

- Newspaper Ads - we've had great success with our newspaper ad. A simple ad drawing the attention of the landlord saying something like: Attention Landlords - We can rent your house for 3-5 years. Guaranteed Rents is perfect!

- Flyers / Postcards in shop windows. You'd be surprised how many people read all those flyers and advertisements in shop windows. So walk through your target area and pop into the local shops and ask them if you can advertise there. Most of them are around £1 per week. Again - keep it simple like in the newspaper ad and use bright colours that will stand out.

- Direct to Landlord letters. This is a more advanced method so we won't go into all the details, but all you need to do is contact your local council for their list of licensed HMOs and their owners. Then you can mail them directly asking if they would be interested in long-term guaranteed rents.

Those are the top forms of marketing that I recommend and have used myself. Keep calm and pick one or two to focus on. And also make sure you don't switch and change too often. Marketing can take some time to build momentum and is all about building trust with your potential clients. I recommend you get a direct marketing method up and running and while that is in the background gaining momentum - get out there are build relationships with agents!

In the next chapeter we are going to be focusing on my other favorite topic: Setting Up Your Systems. I'll give you some great tips on a few key metrics you should be tracking and easy ways to track them!

Chapter 5: Setting Up Your Systems

Once your marketing is setup and the leads are starting to come through. You'll need to start setting up your systems.

The first system is your lead tracking and conversion. This can be a simple spreadsheet and on it you will want to track each lead that comes in, where the lead came from, and what the status of it is. This will help you understand which marketing methods are working best for you.

For example if you have a newspaper ad running for 6 months and only receive one phone call while your postcards from 1 of the corner shops has generated 50 phone calls and 4 deals, then you will likely want to consider changing your newspaper ad or cancelling it all together. But if you aren't tracking this information then you won't know how to tweak it to make it even better (remember in the last email I said that you never give up - only make educated decisions and this is how you make those educated decisions).

The next system you will want is a property tracking for once you start setting up your Rent to Rents.

For tracking bills, tenants, maintenance and more. Again, this can be as simple as excel spreadsheets, especially when you are just getting started, or build up to CRM systems. We use a great free CRM system called Podio to do all of these things. Podio is a free online software that lets you build (or borrow) apps to do exactly what you need to do, custom to your business. Setting up a CRM system takes some time in the beginning but once it's setup it can track things almost effortlessly.

Also you'll want to start thinking about your team. What's the best way of communicating and sharing information with them? You'll want to look at cloud storage, and task lists. I've found an app called Wunderlist which is great for my handyman. It's an app on our mobiles and I simply write down the task I want him to do and it pops up on his phone app. Then when he's completed it he can mark it off and I get a notification saying it's done. Simples :)

Without the proper systems in place you will never have a business that you can run from anywhere in the world and you will always be tied to your business. Basically you will have given yourself another job. You need systems so that you can easily pass over responsibility and tasks to others and know that your business is running just as smoothly as it would if you were there doing it!

Chapter 6
Finding Your Power Team

These are key people like Accountants, Bookkeepers, Solicitors and Insurance Brokers who can recommend the right services for your personal circumstances. These are the professionals that know the details of their profession and can advise you so that you don't have to know everything!

It's always best to have a few people ready from the very start so that you aren't trying to figure it all out from scratch on the day you get the keys to your first rent to rent property. So spend some time finding the people you want to work with. The best way to do this is ask people that are already operating in your area. So head to your local property networking meeting and talk to other landlords and investors and ask them for recommendations!

My biggest tip is to make sure you use people that understand property investing, and preferably are investors themselves!

One of the things that leaders are often pondering is the performance and relationships of their team. Performance indicators show that effective teams will almost always outperform people working individually, particularly in high-pressure situations or when multiple skillsets are needed.

This shouldn't come as much of a surprise, as most organizations are recognizing the importance of team building and are trying to foster it in the workplace. However, building effective teams requires more than an abstract commitment to teamwork; it requires input from managers to foster it.

Without team building skills, a manager risks limiting the productivity of their employees to what each member can do on their own, whereas if you foster team building you can unite your team around a common goal, which will raise productivity as a result.

So here are five steps to building a productive and effective team:

Step 1: Establish leadership.

Before you can start team building, you need to develop the right kind of leadership skills. This doesn't mean asserting authority, instead try to foster trust through honesty and transparency. Especially in larger organizations, managers can't be everywhere at once, but if your employees trust your judgements they will work effectively even when you're not around.

Step 2: Establish relationships with each of your employees.

Try to learn more about each member of your team, their skill sets, how they are motivated and their likes and dislikes. This knowledge is invaluable to leaders, as it allows them to match each employee's expertise and competencies to specific problems, which will help increase their productivity and job satisfaction.

As well as this, try to include your employees in the decision making process where possible. Instead of delegating tasks, give your team's open-ended projects and allow them to determine the best solution. This will encourage them to cooperate and develop problem solving skills.

Step 3: Build relationships between your employees.

As your team starts to cooperate more, examine the way they work together and take steps to improve communication, cooperation and trust amongst the team. If there are any conflicts, try to resolve them amicably. Listen to both sides of the argument and act as a mediator. One way to do this is to brainstorm solutions, which helps to empower your employees and may lead to new solutions to the problem.

Step 4: Foster teamwork.

Once you have established relations with and between your employees, it's time to help them work together effectively. Encourage your team to share information, both amongst themselves and within the wider organisation. Also, try to communicate more with your team. This goes beyond simply holding meetings, and includes things like being open to suggestions and concerns, asking about each team member's work and offering assistance where necessary, and doing everything you can to communicate clearly and honestly with your team.

Step 5: Set ground rules for the team.

Finally, you can begin officially establishing your team through creating team values and goals, as well as evaluating team performance alongside individual performance. Be sure to include your team in this process, so they know what's required and agree with it.

Team building is one of the most important responsibilities a manager has. It isn't something that can be achieved in a short time and then forgotten. It is an ongoing organic process that you a will have to facilitate and guide. As this process unfolds, however, your team members will begin to trust and support one another and share their skill sets and effort in order to more effectively complete your organisation's goals.

Chapter 7
Taking Action!

You may be thinking this step is obvious but this is THE KEY step that most people miss - and that's why it's on here. Most people get so caught up in the details and the learning and research that they never get started. They read a book, watch just one more webinar, or put up just one more test advert, or tweak their direct mail letters just one more time and never actually send them out or go and look at any properties.

Do you know people like that?

Or maybe you've been one of them in the past?

This is the step where you tell yourself:

"I know enough to get started and I'm going to take action today"

Remember that "Better Done than Perfect"

And then just get out there and do it! Take the plunge, get out of your comfort zone and start looking at properties and talking to real people (agents and landlords).

As I mentioned before, you'll never get any Rent to Rents if you don't get out there and start looking at houses and doing viewings. So get out there and do it.

And if you are still too scared to talk to your local agents or landlords and are afraid of messing up the first time - then just do the first few in a different area - pop over to the town or city next door. That way if you mess up it doesn't matter. This will give you a chance to practice speaking and explaining what you are doing without the pressure as you don't really want properties in those areas and if you mess up you never have to see that agent again. So even if you are petrified get out there and do it.

The more you take action and practice the easier it becomes. I didn't get a deal from the first properties I looked at or the first lead that I got. Far from it. I had to talk to quite a few people before I got comfortable explaining it to others so that they had the confidence to do business with me. So start practicing now!!! You have enough information and the next step is to learn by doing!

www.ingramcontent.com/pod-product-compliance
Lightning Source LLC
Chambersburg PA
CBHW031003180726
47993CB00018B/1537